BY THE POWER OF

THEIR DREAMS

▲ ▲

▼ ▼

BY THE POWER OF THEIR DREAMS

Songs, Prayers, and Sacred Shields of the Plains Indians

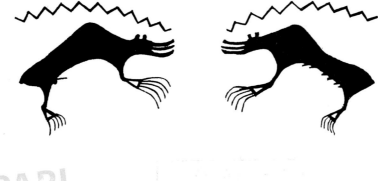

By

Maureen E. Mansell

CHRONICLE BOOKS

SAN FRANCISCO

Grateful acknowledgment is made to the copyright holders for permission to reprint or adapt from the following sources.

Arapaho prayer, "Listen All You Creatures," reprinted courtesy of The Wind River Rendezvous, Saint Stephen's Indian Mission Foundation, Wyoming.

Cheyenne songs, "My Grandfather the Sun" and "Song of Turtle," from Cheyenne and Arapaho Music: Southwest Museum Papers 10, by Frances Densmore. Copyright © 1936, reprinted courtesy of the Southwest Museum, Los Angeles, California.

Cheyenne legend, "Wolf Man and His Daughter," from The Wolves of Heaven: Cheyenne Shamanism, Ceremonies, and Prehistoric Origins, by Karl H. Schlesier. Copyright © 1987 by the University of Oklahoma Press. Permission granted.

Crow prayer, "My Sorrows Are Many," from Crow Prayers by R. H. Lowie. Reproduced by permission of the American Anthropological Association from American Anthropologist 35, 1933.

Kiowa song, "I Live but I Will Not Live Forever," from Kiowa Years: A Study in Culture Impact, by Alice Marriott, 1968. Reprinted courtesy of MacMillan McGraw. Copyright © 1968, by MacMillan McGraw Publishing Co.

Sioux quote, "Surrounded with Blessings," from Land of the Spotted Eagle, by Chief Luther Standing Bear (Houghton Mifflin, 1933). Reprinted with permission of Geoffrey Standing Bear.

Sioux commentary, "On Seeking a Vision," by George Sword. Reprinted from Lakota Belief and Ritual, by James R. Walker, edited by Raymond J. DeMallie and Elaine A. Jahner, by permission of the University of Nebraska Press. Copyright © 1980, 1991 by the University of Nebraska Press. Permission also granted to reprint the extract "Behold the Sacred Hoop" from The Sixth Grandfather:

Black Elk's Teachings Given to John G. Neihardt, ed. by Raymond J. DeMallie, University of Nebraska Press, 1984.

Sioux quote from "The Vision Quest" by Lame Deer, in American Indian Myths and Legends, edited by Richard Erdoes and Alfonso Ortiz. Copyright © 1983 by Richard Erdoes and Alfonso Ortiz. Reprinted by permission of Pantheon Books, a division of Random House, Inc.

Every effort has been made to trace the copyright holders and obtain required permissions. If any acknowledgments have been omitted or rights overlooked, the author asks forgiveness, and if notified, will endeavor to include the corrections in future printings.

Printed in Hong Kong.

Library of Congress Cataloging-in-Publication Data
Mansell, Maureen E.
    By the power of their dreams : songs, prayers, and sacred shields of the Plains Indians / by Maureen E. Mansell.
        p.   cm.
    Includes bibliographical references.
    ISBN 0-8118-0460-7
    1. Indians of North America—Great Plains—Religion and mythology.
    2. Indian poetry—Great Plains—Translations into English.
    3. Indians of North America—Great Plains—Arms and armor.
    4. Shields—Great Plains. I. Title.
E78.G73M35   1994
299'.798—dc20   93-8148
                                                        CIP

Line editing: Suzanne Kotz
Book and cover design: Julie Noyes Long

Distributed in Canada by Raincoast Books,
112 East Third Avenue, Vancouver, B.C. V5T 1C8

10 9 8 7 6 5 4 3 2 1

Chronicle Books
275 Fifth Street
San Francisco, CA 94103

Dedicated to the Native American people of the Great Plains, past and present.

ACKNOWLEDGMENTS

For the opportunities to research the shields given by courtesy of the museums and private collections, with work space generously provided, I wish to thank Gerald Conaty and Dennis Slater of the Glenbow Museum, Calgary; Richard Haas and Horst Wedell of the Museum für Völkerkunde, Berlin; Christine Gross of the Field Museum, Chicago; H. Malcolm Grimmer of Morning Star Gallery, Santa Fe; Jonathan King of the Museum of Mankind, London; John Rubenstein and Deborah Wood of the Smithsonian Institution, Washington, D.C.; and the curators of the Philbrook Museum.

I am especially grateful to Andrew Hunter Whiteford of the School of American Research for his enthusiastic interest and invaluable help. My thanks are due also to Alexander Acevedo, Richard Conn, Paul Dyck, Laura Holt, George Horse Capture, Dale Idiens, Ronald McCoy, Alfonso Ortiz, Nathaniel Owings, Joyce Szabo, Bill Swift, and Donald Cushman. I would like to express my appreciation, particularly to Charlotte Stone, to all the people at Chronicle Books who gave continued support and expertise.

A special thank you goes to J. Fraser Mansell for his research assistance, and to Gordon Mansell, who gave encouragement, shared the journey, and rallied forces along the way.

CONTENTS
▼ ▼ ▼ ▼ ▼ ▼ ▼ ▼ ▼ ▼

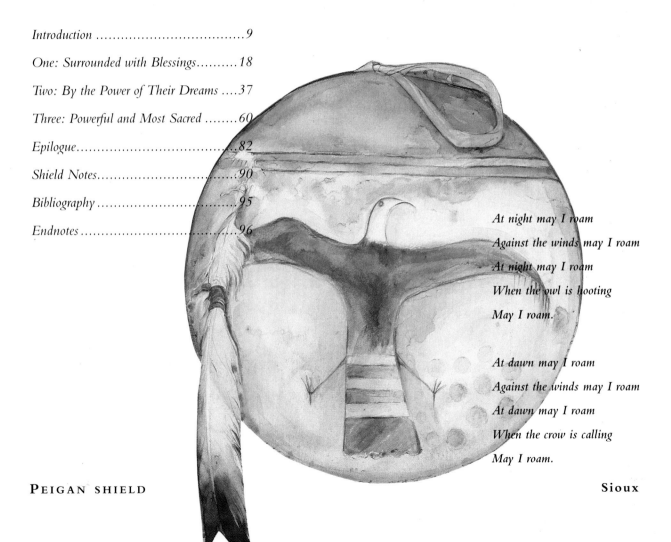

PEIGAN SHIELD

At night may I roam
Against the winds may I roam
At night may I roam
When the owl is hooting
May I roam.

At dawn may I roam
Against the winds may I roam
At dawn may I roam
When the crow is calling
May I roam.

Sioux

AUTHOR'S NOTE

When I lived for many years near the Rocky Mountains, where they rise from the prairie, I often wondered about the people who had passed that way before. Not the trappers or gold miners, but the Native Americans who followed the buffalo across the Great Plains and sometimes wintered in the canyons near present-day Boulder, Colorado. Wild berries grew alongside our old creek, and deer came down to browse under the cottonwoods during snowstorms. It was easy to imagine an Arapaho encampment in this sheltered place, a small band with their chief, Left-Hand, whose name now graces nearby landmarks. Wanting to know more, I read their myths and legends, and searched ethnographies on other Plains Indians—the Cheyenne and Sioux, Blackfeet, Crow and Pawnee, and the Comanches and Kiowas of the southern Plains. In American Indian art collections I saw buffalo hide transformed into tipi covers, moccasins, shirts, and dresses of great beauty. But it was warriors' shields that riveted my attention, with their symbolic images of remarkable color and form, painted from dreams and visions. I knew that shields often became the trophies of explorers and soldiers, and that hundreds of shields must have been made at the height of Plains culture, but relatively few are on public view. In 1984 I started to trace others, writing to museums in North America and Europe, arranging to visit, record, and make detailed drawings of authentic shields in their collections. How strange it was, in a museum in Berlin, to be holding a worn Arapaho shield, removed from its dark storage drawer so many thousands of miles from its origin, yet still a testament to the owner's bravery and wisdom.

Many of the items I found were fragile and faded, or had motifs lost beneath thick pendants of feathers. I began to preserve the images in watercolor paintings that remained true to the original quality of the buffalo hide designs. At the same time I gathered Plains Indian songs and prayers, and fragments of nineteenth-century texts that seemed in harmony with the paintings. By showing images and verses together, I wanted to convey something of the aesthetic and spiritual quality that permeated the lives of the Plains people. Instead of the sad theme of a vanishing race, the shields and verses speak of the great cycle of renewal and regeneration in life.

THE
SACRED CIRCLE

◆ ◆ ◆

THE SACRED CIRCLE

The sun and the sky, the earth and the moon are round
like a shield, though the sky is deep like a bowl.
Everything that breathes is round like the body of a man.
Everything that grows from the ground is round
like the stem of a tree. Since the Great Spirit has caused
everything to be round, mankind should look upon the
circle as sacred for it is the symbol of all things except
stone. It is also the symbol of the circle that marks the
edge of the world and therefore of the four winds that
travel there. . . . The day, the night, and the moon go in a
circle above the sky. Therefore the circle is a symbol of
these divisions of time and the symbol of all time.

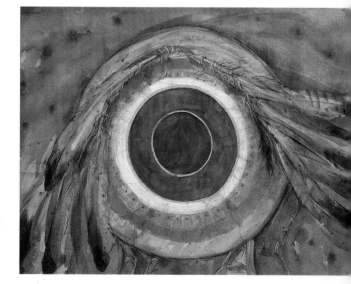

Sioux

INTRODUCTION

Beneath the encircling sky, when vast herds of buffalo still covered the open prairie stretching westward from the Missouri River to the Rocky Mountains, horse-mounted Indians of the Great Plains followed a nomadic, hunting way of life that found unique expression in their artistic tradition. With supreme skill they crafted from the materials at hand—animal hides, porcupine quills, earth pigments, feathers, and fur—their robes and horse trappings, headdresses, and ceremonial objects of sacred power.

Among the most highly prized items of a Plains warrior's regalia was the beautifully painted buffalo-hide shield. A shield deflected arrows in battle, but its greatest value lay in the personal protection afforded by its supernatural design. Received by a warrior in a dream or vision during a spiritual quest, shield imagery was a testimonial to his spirit mentor and represented the careful recording of a revelation sent by the sacred powers who presided over the destiny and well-being of the tribe.

The nomadic Plains Indian culture in the early nineteenth century revolved around the seasonal hunt of the buffalo. In search of migrating herds that grazed the land, the people moved from one hunting ground to another, according to the time of year and their knowledge of the territory.

Traveling in small bands, they transported their entire belongings, household goods, and movable tipis to each new encampment, which again became an organized center of daily life. From the buffalo came everything needed to sustain them for many months ahead, and a successful hunt was an occasion for feasting and celebration. Then began the hard work of processing meat and curing the valuable skins. Hides, either tanned or left natural, replaced worn tipi covers and clothing, and were fashioned into saddle bags and storage containers for dried meat, tobacco, weapons, and war bonnets. The thick hide needed for a warrior's shield was cut from the toughest portion of an old bull's shoulder. Every part of this immense animal was preserved, including the buffalo skull, which assumed an important place in special ceremonies of gratitude and petition to the benevolent powers for ensuring the continued abundance of the herds.

In Plains society a young man was prepared from early childhood for his dual role as warrior and provider. While his first duty lay in facing the considerable dangers of the buffalo hunt, he also was trained in the skilled art of horse raiding and in the warrior's code. Within the strict re-quirements of the Plains Indian ethic, a man was expected to strive for honors in battle and to bravely confront his enemies. Honesty and generosity, devotion to duty, and selfless deeds on behalf of his people were the traditional ways to gain respect and status. Usually a boy was guided and instructed by an esteemed older man, often an uncle or brother, who took dutiful pride in helping the youngster attain maturity.

Life on the Plains was one of hardship and sacrifice, and often balanced at the edge of subsistence. The warrior's path was fraught with physical danger, which at the peak of manhood he actively pursued, spurred on by the challenges and risks of war. He sought the protection and power to carry him through life from an ever-present spiritual plane, made accessible to him through visions and dreams.

In the old tribal world, supernatural power permeated Plains Indian experience, infusing the everyday lives of the people with symbolic meaning and sacred purpose. In the ongoing cycle of birth, death, and renewal, animals central to physical survival were revered as the agents of seen or unseen spirit forces controlling the universe. Movement of the stars, waxing and waning of the moon, and the changing seasons beneath the life-generating sun all revealed the presence of the supreme powers who shaped the course of human events and blessed those who lived in a sacred manner.

Vision quests to bring long life and harmony with these omnipotent powers were a respected custom among all the Plains tribes. Men and women alike sought supernatural guidance and strength throughout life's difficulties and transitions, as at the death of a relative or friend, or the birth of a child. Sacred designs originating in dreams were sewn by women onto dresses, moccasins, and baby carriers, and most bead and quill work carried religious significance. Shields were men's special property, associated with the warpath and the protection of the tribe from its enemies. When a warrior's dream image was transcribed onto the shield or its soft outer cover, it was invariably done by a man.

Only those men who were proven worthy received a vision. Too potent for direct communication, such sacred knowledge was acquired through contact with the messengers of the powers who, at the moment of encounter, were mysteriously able to make themselves understood in human terms. Appearing in animal, bird, or celestial forms, they brought gifts of wisdom, a song of power, or instructions for strength and safety to show the beneficiary how to act in times of danger or hardship. The imagery on a warrior's shield was painted from these sources to honor and represent the benefactors from the spirit world. In turn, a reciprocal protection often existed; in the ancient Cheyenne laws, for example, every person blessed by the adoption of a supernatural guardian also accepted responsibility for the species that symbolized it.

Making the shield called for solemn ritual. Usually the holy powers of a tribal elder imparted the necessary spiritual quality to aid the owner in expressing his visionary experience in a tangible and enduring form. When he painted the visual shape of his spirit messenger, it was not simply a representation of its power, it was the cosmic power. In this way a warrior acquired the sacred gift that rendered him invulnerable and powerful—mysteries beyond ordinary understanding and first called "medicine" by French voyageurs. Portrayed in earth colors of symbolic value, shield imagery might also depict lightning, clouds, hail, and thunder, weather conditions that sometimes accompanied the appearance of spirit messengers. Because of the personal nature of dreams, however, designs and motifs could be accurately interpreted only by those who created the shields or by relatives who inherited them. On occasion, members of a man's own warrior society who had witnessed the "proving" of a shield's medicine during a horse raid or military campaign might feel qualified to relate its history. But most shield imagery embodied complex layers of meaning and ritual purpose that varied according to a man's innermost beliefs.

The sacred forces surrounding the creation of medicine shields and the sense of mystery attached to them are best expressed in the powerful words of their own people. The accompanying texts are drawn from the Arapaho, Cheyenne, and Sioux of the central plains; the northern Blackfoot, the Crow, and eastern plains Pawnee; and the Kiowa and Comanche of the southern grasslands. Many were collected by pioneering nineteenth-century ethnologists, who worked to preserve the oral histories of a buffalo-hunting culture undergoing the devastating changes of a developing continent. The voices of Brave Buffalo, Lone Man, Humped-Wolf, and

Eagle Chief, along with many unknown warriors, speak on matters that are sometimes inexplicable to the non-Indian mind. Their songs, prayers, and commentaries give poetic insight into the sanctity of their traditional world and enhance our respectful appreciation of the intangible spirit of Plains Indian shields.

SONG FOR SECURING FAIR WEATHER

May the Sun rise well!
May the earth appear
Brightly shone upon.

May the Moon rise well!
May the earth appear
Brightly shone upon.

Sioux

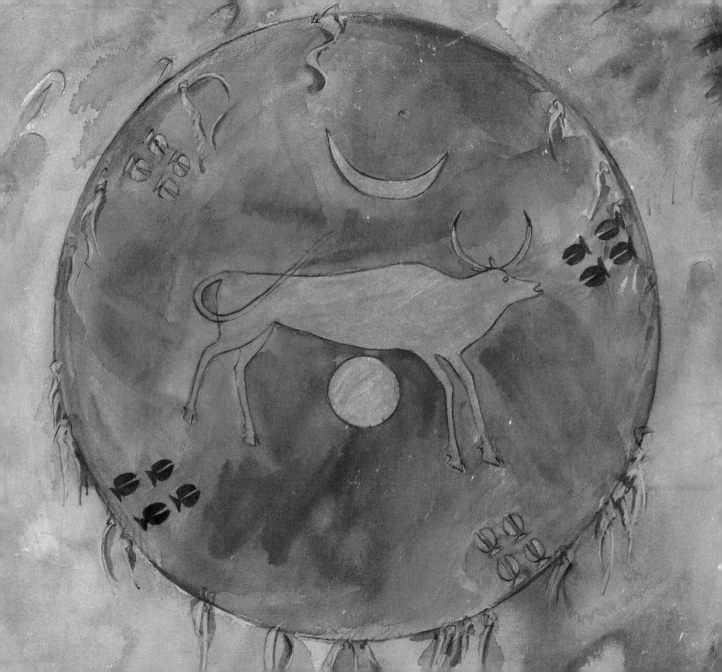

PRAYER OF AN ELDER
FOR A YOUNG MAN'S START IN LIFE

My grandfather, the Sun, you who walk yellow,
Look down on us. Pity us. Pity us.
May this young man facing straight
Be helped to walk for his life!

Those that shine above at night,
And the animals of the night, we pray to you.
The Morning Star, and my Father, listen!
I have asked for long breath, for large life.

May this young man, with his people and his relatives do well,
Walking where it is good, obtaining food and clothing,
And horses of many colors, and where birds are calling,
And the day is long and the wind is good.

Arapaho

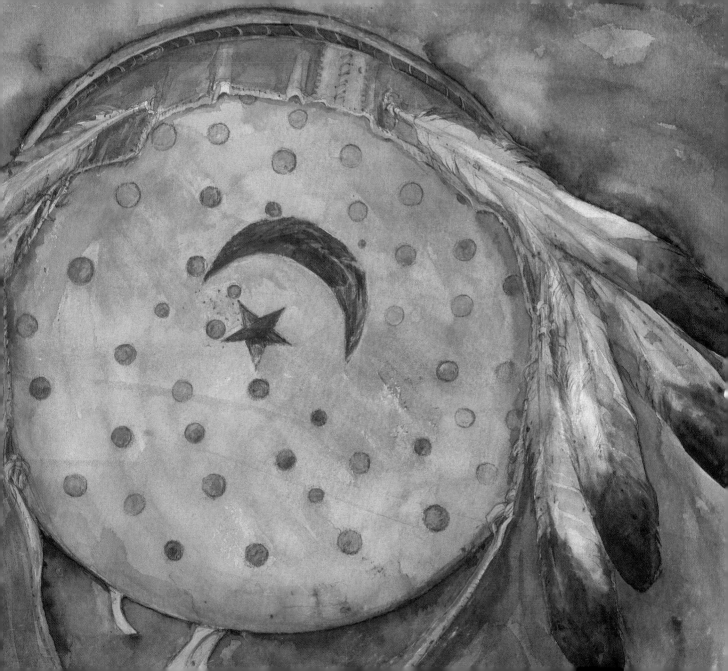

CHAPTER ONE

SURROUNDED WITH
BLESSINGS

****

SURROUNDED WITH BLESSINGS
BELIEF AND RITUAL

*In the beginning of all things, wisdom and
knowledge were with the animals, for Tirawa,
the One Above, did not speak directly to man.
He sent certain animals to tell men that he
showed himself through the beasts, and from
them and from the stars and the sun and the
moon man should learn. Tirawa spoke to man
through his works, and the Pawnee
understands the heavens, the beasts, and the plants.
For all things tell of Tirawa.*

Pawnee

The Cheyennes tell an ancient story of how they first came to hold a sacred kinship with the animals. They were camping in the tall grass country, far from their own lands. The all-powerful Wolf Man sent his own daughter, Yellow-Haired Woman, to the Cheyenne camp with a special mission: "Those poor people have only fish and a few birds to eat, but now you are there, there will be plenty of game of all kinds and the skins of these animals will also be useful for wearing." And Yellow-Haired Woman became the master spirit of the animals, and through her power she brought game to the Cheyennes. The buffalo came up to their lodge and rubbed themselves against it, and all the hidden animals of the Plains followed and let themselves be killed.

Indian tradition abounds with legends of animal powers. For the horse-mounted hunters of the Plains who followed the grazing herds, life was inseparably linked with the natural world. They saw themselves and all other manifestations of the life force as participants in an eternal cycle of transformation and renewal. Animals were revered as mystical and powerful: they were benevolent sources of practical instruction, essential food, and spirit-power, yet they were equal partners in the drama of survival with whom the covenant of life for life must be maintained. Tribal ceremonies, celebrating the beautiful and mysterious workings of their world, honored the communion with the animals and with the omnipotent powers, the Sun, and the Four Winds. Underlying their affinity with the natural environment, at the heart of Indian philosophy, lay a deeply rooted belief in the spiritual unity of the universe.

Centered around the great hunt, Plains Indian culture evolved as a dynamic expression of the people's interrelationships with animals and the forces of the natural environment. Amidst vast and seemingly empty prairies, they created a pattern of life that held spiritual purpose and provided the practical means of survival—a life rooted in the land they honored as the domain of the spirit forms of animals, birds, plants, and all things bestowed by the powers to sustain life. Everything thus created was recognized as sacred and meaningful, and a potential source of spiritual aid. In the words of Chief Luther Standing Bear of the Oglala Sioux: "We did not think of the great open plains, the beautiful rolling hills, and the winding streams with tangled growth as wild. Only to the white man was nature a wilderness and only to him was the land infested with wild animals and savage people. To us it was tame. Earth was bountiful and we were surrounded with blessings of the Great Mystery."

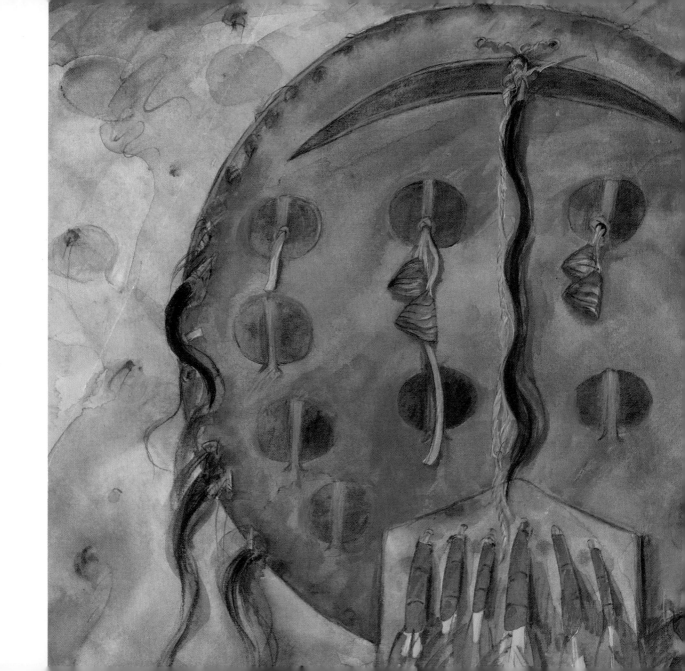

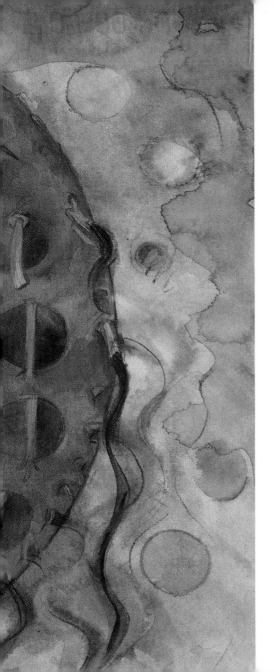

MAN MUST DO THE GREATER PART

I have noticed in my life that all men have a
liking for some special animal, tree, plant,
or spot of earth. If men would pay more
attention to these preferences and seek what
is best to do in order to make themselves
worthy . . . they might have dreams which
would purify their lives. Let a man decide
upon his favorite animal and make a study of
it, learning its innocent ways. Let him learn
to understand its sounds and motions. The
animals want to communicate with man, but
Wakan Tanka does not intend they shall do so
directly—man must do the greater part in
securing understanding.

Brave Buffalo, Sioux

PLEASING THE SPIRITS

There are spirits belonging to places and things,
to animals, birds, and all creatures.
The spirit of the earth is most powerful,
and the spirit of the rock; next the spirit of the buffalo
is most powerful; it has control over love, procreation,
and the family, and also the hunt.
The spirit of the eagle governs over councils, hunters,
and war parties. The spirit of the thunder governs the
weather, the clouds, and the rain. . . .
The power of the spirit should be honored with its color.
Red is the color of the sun;
but it is too powerful and will not be a spirit
to any person. Blue is the color of the spirits of the sky
and the Four Winds. Green is the color of the spirit
of the earth. The colors are the same for the friends
of the Great Spirits.
A man who paints red is pleasing to them. . . .
The influence of the spirits is everywhere, all the time.

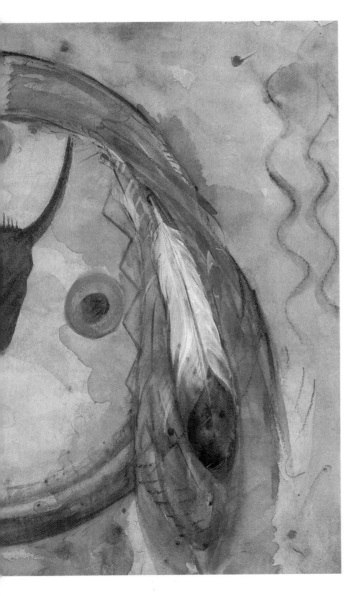

If the spirits cannot come when they are called,
their messengers will act for them.
A medicine man knows what songs to sing,
and what is pleasing to the spirits.
The smoke of the sweet grass pleases the good spirits;
the smoke of the sage will drive bad spirits away.

Sioux

CIRCLE OF THE SKY

Remember, remember the circle of the sky

> the stars and the brown eagle
> the supernatural winds
> breathing night and day
> for the four directions.

Remember, remember the great life of the sun

> breathing on the earth
> it lies upon the earth
> to bring out life upon the earth,
> life covering the earth.

Pawnee

LISTEN ALL YOU CREATURES

Listen . . .
All you creatures
        under the ground,
All you creatures
        above the ground
        and in the waters.
May this people
        be long in life,
        and increase.
May our boys and girls,
        our children of all ages . . .
May our grown men and women,
        and all our elders . . .
May they increase
        and be strengthened.

Arapaho

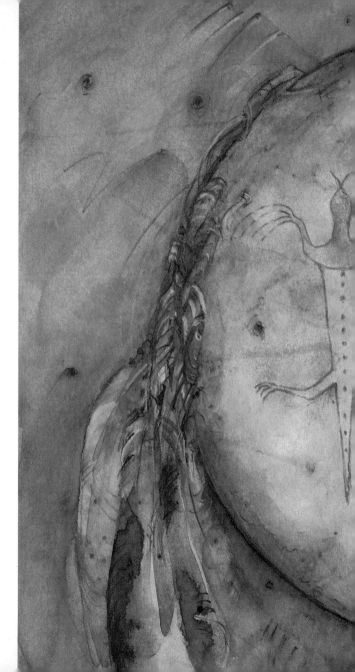

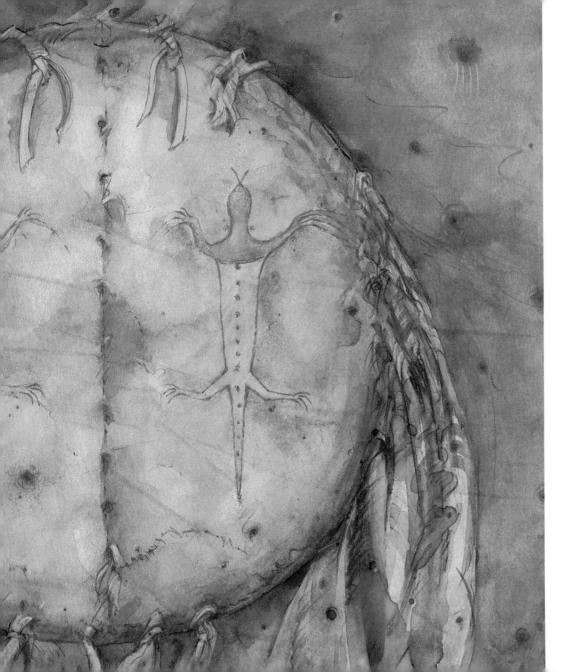

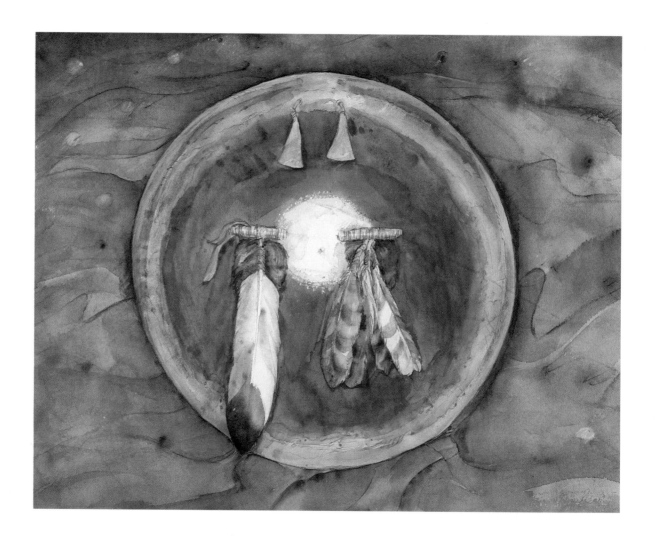

30 ✳✳✳✳

MAY THE WINTER BE GOOD

Greeting Sun! I have made this robe for you, that my living may be good.

May I and my people safely reach the next year.

My children, may they increase; my sons on the warpath,

May they return with horses, and with faces painted black.

When I am on the move, may the wind come to my face,

May the buffalo gather towards me.

This summer, may my plants be good, may the cherries be plentiful.

May I see the new grass and the full grown leaves when they come.

May the winter be good, may illness not reach me.

May I and my people all safely reach the spring.

Crow

PRAYER TO THE SUN

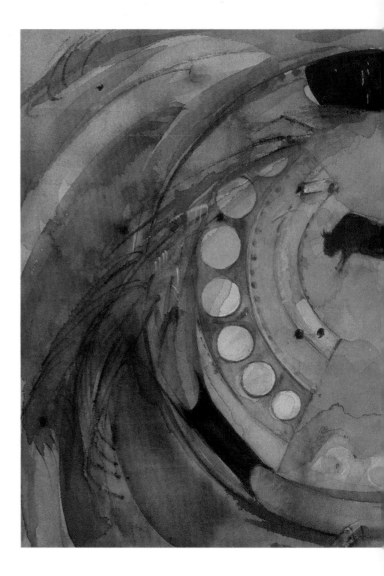

Iyo!

Sun, take pity on me; take pity on me.

Old age, old age, we are praying to your old age,

For that I have chosen.

Your children, morning star, seven stars,

The bunched stars, these and all stars,

We call upon them for help.

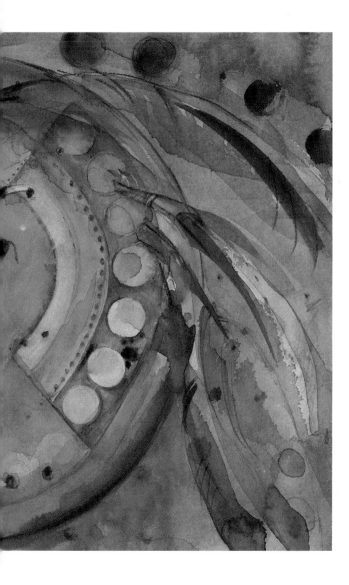

Iyo!

Take pity on me that I may lead a good life.

My children, now I have led them to old age.

Now you above people, I have called upon you for help;

Good days and happy nights, for those I have called.

You must listen to me; take pity on me.

Old age, let me lead my children to it,

Iyo!

Blackfoot

SPEECH BY TEN BEARS
(Extract)

I was born on the prairie

Where the wind blew free,

And there was nothing to break the light of the sun.

I was born where there were no enclosures

And where everything drew a free breath.

I want to die there, and not within walls.

Comanche

THAT WIND

That wind, that wind

        Shakes my tipi, shakes my tipi,

And sings a song for me,

        And sings a song for me.

Kiowa

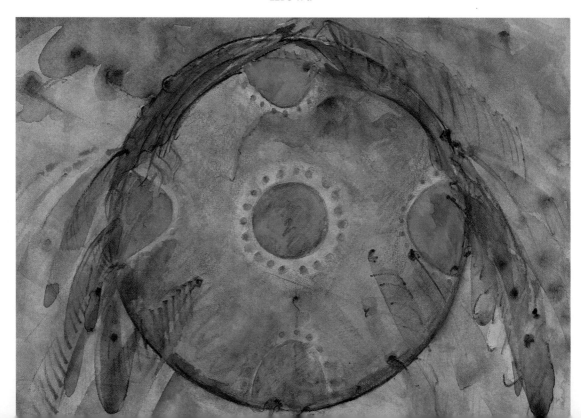

CHAPTER SEVEN

BY THE
POWER OF THEIR
DREAMS

▲▲▲▲

BY THE POWER OF THEIR DREAMS
THE VISION QUEST

The Creator of the Blackfoot world, Napi, told the people:
"Now, if you are overcome, you may go to sleep, and get power.
Something will come to you in your dream, that will help you.
Whatever these animals tell you to do, you must obey them,
as they appear to you in your sleep.
Be guided by them.
If anyone wants help, if you are alone and traveling, and cry aloud for help,
your prayer will be answered.
It may be by the eagles, perhaps by the buffalo, or by the bears.
That was how the first people got through the world,
by the power of their dreams."

Blackfoot

CHAPTER TWO

Danger of every kind—witnessed in the drama of the great buffalo hunt and in the unrelenting forces of nature—was an accepted condition of life on the Plains. As part of their ongoing struggle for survival, Plains Indian nations relentlessly engaged in intertribal warfare. Without the constraints of established boundaries, their nomadic existence inevitably carried with it the risk of conflict as the people searched for horses and hunting territory. Although the primary purpose of war in all Indian tribes was the protection of weaker members—children and the elderly—setting out on the warpath or a horse raid was also a longed-for opportunity to gain prestige and status. Such expeditions were charged with risk and uncertainty. Excitement rose as a gaming sense of adventure spurred warriors to heroic and often suicidal bids for glory. Gambling and chance played a strong part in the Plains Indian ethos. In one Blackfoot legend, for example, a newly forged peace between Shoshoni and Peigan bands was soon broken when a group of young men played a game that took a serious turn, their youthful competition ending in bloodshed and renewed enmity.

As protector of his people, the Plains warrior sought above all to win honors in battle. Praying for strength and courage, he knew many dangers could be overcome only with the aid of supernatural forces. Vision power, for those who could acquire it, was the mark of maturity and brought benefits to the whole tribe. This code of honor was so strongly upheld by traditional custom that a boy rarely needed persuading to begin the quest for power. From adolescence he was encouraged in this undertaking, usually with the help of a shaman who prepared him for the time of fasting and solitude ahead. Later, if he were successful, the tribal elders would proffer insights on the boy's vision and interpret the special instructions given by the spirit messenger.

Vision quests to bring long life and harmony with the powers of the universe continued throughout adulthood. To show the necessary respect for the powers with prayers and offerings, a man prepared to make his solemn petition by undergoing ritual purification. He set aside the concerns of everyday life and shed the garments and weapons of physical protection. Stripped of his worldly possessions and clad only in a buffalo robe, the warrior departed to an isolated place where he fasted for several days. With mind, body, and spirit cleansed and centered, he became wholly receptive to whatever events and apparitions might occur. His awareness tuned to every sight and sound, he waited for an agent of the powers to recognize him as one in true need of help and guidance.

Yet the enlightenment of a vision and the clarity of a dream, like most inspiration, never came upon demand, for the more consciously the will strives, the harder it becomes for the mind to remain open. Spiritual preparation and contemplation were essential, as were respectful, disciplined attitudes. In one account of a young man's futile attempts, Sioux medicine man Lame Deer tells how an inappropriate quest for power brought admonitions from the elders: " 'Well, you did find out one thing,' said his uncle. 'You went after your vision like a hunter after a buffalo or a warrior after scalps. You were fighting the spirits. You thought they owed you a vision. Suffering alone brings no vision nor does courage, nor does sheer will power. A vision comes as a gift born of humility, of wisdom, and of patience. If from your vision quest you have learned nothing but this, then you have already learned much.' "

ON SEEKING A VISION

No Lakota should undertake anything of great importance without first seeking a vision relative to it. Hanble *(a vision) is a communication from Wakan Tanka or a spirit to one of mankind. It may come at any time or in any manner to anyone. It may be relative to the one who receives it, or to another. It may be communicated in Lakota, or* hanbloglaka *(language of the spirits). Or it may be only by sight or sounds not of a language. It may come directly from the one giving it, or it may be sent by an* akicita *(messenger). It may come unsought for, or it may come by seeking it. To seek a vision one should* inipi *(taking a vapor bath) and then remain alone as much as possible, thinking continually of that about which he desires a vision. While doing this he should eat no food nor take any drink, but he may smoke the pipe. . . .*

If the vision desired is concerning a matter of much importance, a shaman should supervise all the ceremony relative to it. If it is a small matter, there need be but little ceremony, but if it is of very great importance there should be much ceremony. The greatest ceremony is the Sun Dance in order to receive a communication from the Sun. When one receives a communication in a vision he should be governed by it, otherwise Wakan Tanka will bring misfortune upon him.

George Sword, Lakota Sioux

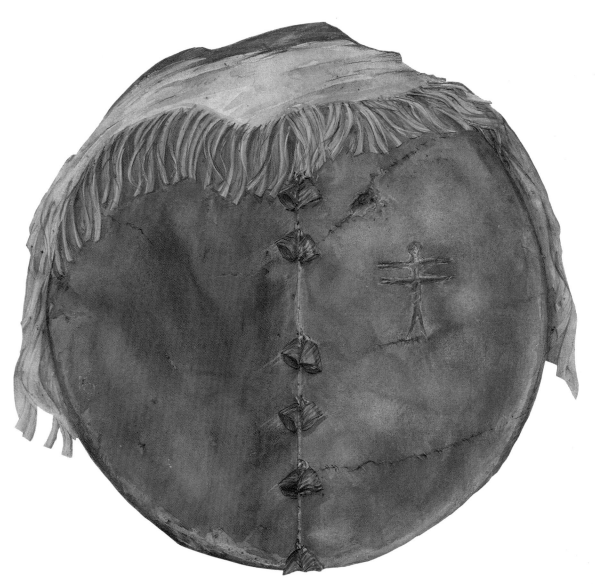

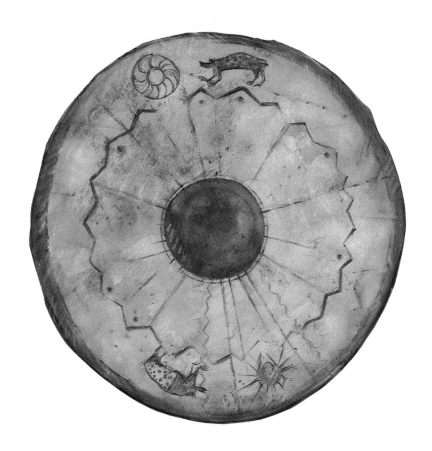

DREAM OF THE WOLVES

When I was about 22 years of age I dreamed that I came to a wolf den and found the little wolves unprotected by either father or mother. They seemed to say, "We are left here helpless, but our parents will soon return." I learned their song. . . . Soon I saw the old wolf returning and behind him came a buffalo calf. This old wolf told me how to make a pipe, telling me to smoke it when I was on the warpath and saying that the smell of the pipe would be so strong that the enemy would not detect my approach and thus I would be able to steal their horses. The old wolf said that by the aid of this pipe I would be able to outwit the wisest and craftiest of my enemies. I made the pipe as he directed and carried it on the warpath and had good success. It did not look any different from an ordinary pipe, but it had been "made sacred" by a medicine-man.

Charging Thunder, Sioux

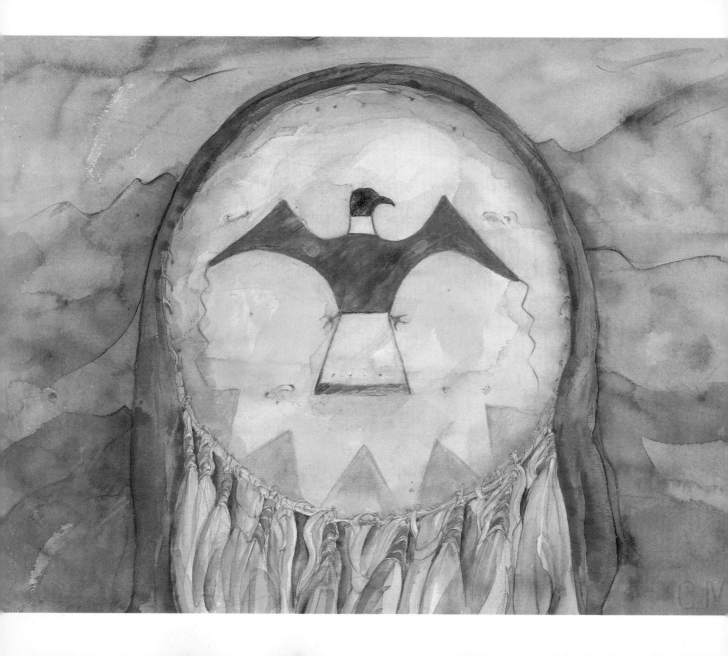

ADDRESS TO THE
MYSTERY POWERS OF THE NORTH

This day no other creatures may be mentioned by you

      Spotted Eagle most powerful

      Lend me this day one of your good days

                                   This boy will renew the life of his people

                                         One of your plumes I borrow

                                         Lend me one of your good days

May the nation live, and may there be no adversity

      Before the face of the North

      Let the nation live.

Sioux

FOUR SPELLS TO BRING SLEEP

In the fall when the drizzle is pattering on the tipi,
And we lie inside with blankets over us,
We can't help falling asleep, can we?

On windy days, when we lie down in a thick hollow
And listen to the rustling in the pine trees,
We soon fall asleep, don't we?

When the day is cloudy, the thunder makes a low rumble
And we hear the rain striking against the tipi,
Then it's nice to sleep, isn't it?

In winter we are out a long time hunting deer,
And when we come back tired to our tipi and find it warm,
We sleep well, don't we?

Crow

WARRIOR SOCIETY SONG

I live, but I will not live forever.

Mysterious moon, you only remain,

Powerful sun, you alone remain,

Wonderful earth, you remain forever . . .

All of us soldiers must die.

Kiowa

A Bear's Prophecy

A young warrior named Raven-face went searching for a vision one winter. Caught in a bad snowstorm, he became soaked to the skin, and when a cold wind began to blow, he could see no way to survive. In desperation he crawled into a bear's cave, and although there were two little cubs there, he lay down beside them and fell asleep exhausted.

In the night the parents returned. When they saw him lying beside their cubs, they did not try to waken him. Next morning when Raven-face awoke, he saw the bears waiting at the entrance. He felt very afraid, and thought that they would devour him. Instead the male bear took him in his arms and sang. Raising him high he said: "Look around. Do you see the whole world, dear child? There is nothing for you to be afraid of in death. Go home, sleep well, and eat. As long as you have teeth you have nothing to fear."

Raven-face's vision took him through many dangerous encounters with his enemies, and in a buffalo hunt at the canyon of the Bighorn he escaped being gored by a wounded bull and trampled over the cliff. It came true what the bear told Raven-face—that he need not fear death until he grew old.

Crow

PRAYER TO THE THUNDER

Okohe! Okohe! Iyo!
Thunder, we beseech you, we beseech you
Help me, help me
Help me in that for which I have called upon you,
For old age, the ability to escape dangers.
Have mercy on me Thunder,
That Wing sign, that food, that good tobacco,
All these have been put away for you
That you may do this for me.

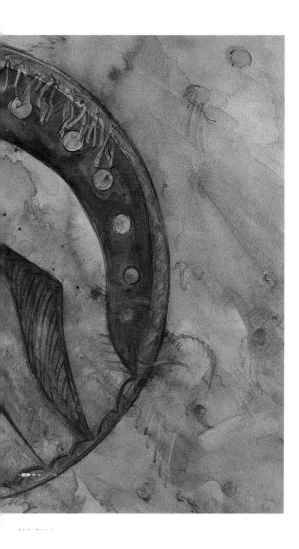

Okohe! Okohe! Iyo!

Have pity on all children and all women,

All the old men, and the middle-aged men, and the married men.

Try to take notice of them, try to take notice of them,

Grant them safety, grant them safety.

We are glad to meet you again for the sake of fortunate days.

For this have mercy on me, for I have chosen many summer days

That I may live happily,

That I may see many snows.

Blackfoot

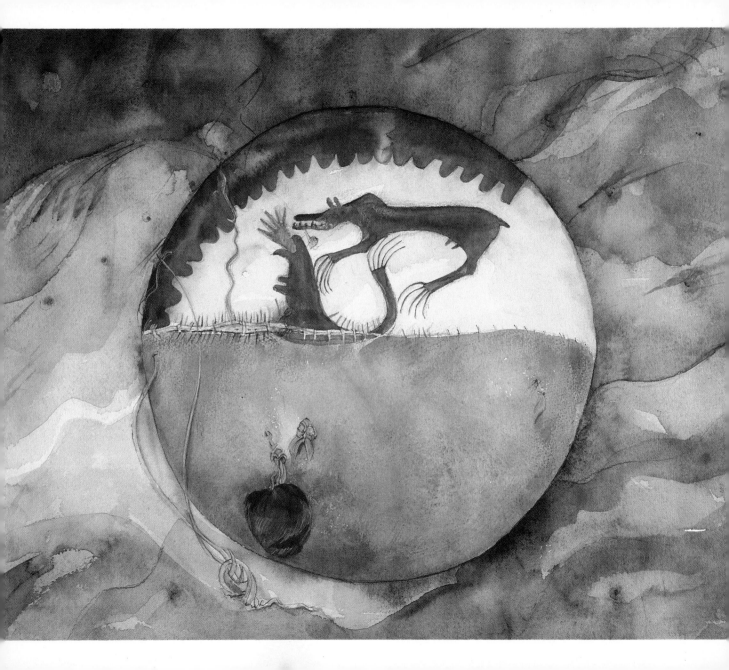

DEATH COMES
AND YOU CANNOT LEAP OVER HIM

When your friends have fear on their faces,

And weep within themselves,

And run this way and that before the enemy,

Stay behind and fight!

Do not come back!

Death comes and you cannot leap over him.

Crow

OFFERING TO THE SPIRITS

He That Hears Always, hear my cries!
As my tears drop to the ground, look upon me.
Spirits, I give you this, my body.
May I have many horses, and many women
of beauty and industry in my lodge.
May my lodge be the gathering place of men.
I am poor. Give me those things that
through me my people may be strong because I live.
Let them use me as a shield against the enemy!

Crow

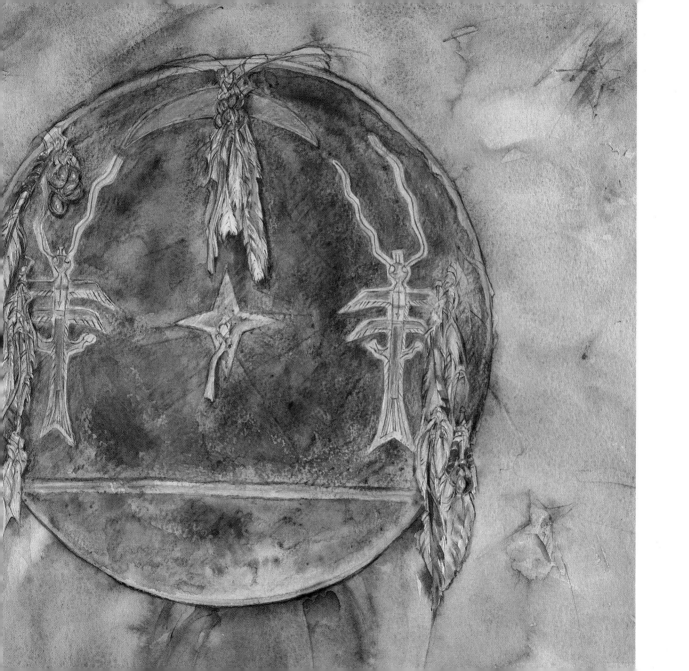

◇ ◇

CHAPTER THREE

POWERFUL

AND

MOST SACRED

◇ ◇ ◇ ◇

POWERFUL AND MOST SACRED
MEDICINE SHIELDS

From Wakan Tanka, the Great Mystery, comes all power. It is from Wakan Tanka that the holy man has wisdom and the power to heal, and to make sacred charms. Man knows that all healing plants are given by Wakan Tanka; therefore they are holy. So too is the buffalo sacred, because it is the gift of Wakan Tanka. The Great Mystery gave to men all things for their food, their clothing, and their welfare. And to man he gave also the knowledge how to use these gifts—how to find the holy healing plants, how to hunt and surround the buffalo, how to know wisdom. For all comes from Wakan Tanka—all.

Sioux

CHAPTER THREE

For the Plains warrior, a vision brought the sacred gift of medicine, a blessing from supernatural sources that took many forms—the power to heal, to prophesy, to be invulnerable in battle, to be successful in hunting. From this blessing the warrior gained a profound confidence that he would be guided to accomplish great deeds and to protect his people's well-being. In return, the warrior was to honor the powers and to re-create in some tangible form the spirit messengers who appeared in his dream. Their images, when painted on the warrior's shield, symbolized the revered possession of sacred knowledge. Only a man of outstanding courage and integrity could own a medicine shield, and only he could reproduce the special symbols given for his protection.

Painting the design was usually directed and sometimes executed by a tribal elder with spiritual status—one whose knowledge of the mysteries could safeguard the shield's medicine and ensure its owner's favorable relationship with the powers. As with all religious items, strict rules surrounded the proper use and handling of shields. Varying according to individual belief or tribal custom, these restrictions maintained harmony among the potent forces of the earth, sun, and moon, or any other power with which they might conflict.

The sacred task of constructing a shield from raw buffalo hide, shrunk to a desired thickness and size over a fire pit, could also require a holy man's assistance. The early explorers Lewis and Clark observed Shoshoni Indians conducting a shield forming ceremony, and a historic journal entry for August 23, 1805, by Meriwether Lewis notes that "this implement would in their minds be divested of much of its protecting power were it not inspired with those virtues by their older men. . . . Many believe that a [musket] ball cannot penetrate their shields in consequence of certain supernatural powers."

In the early nineteenth century warriors commonly carried shields on the warpath, where their practical value in combat was considerable. Rendered hard and impenetrable after many hours pegged over hot embers, a shield afforded protection against arrows, lances, or clubs. Its solid hide was heavy enough to deflect even the ball of an old smooth bore rifle. After the introduction of heavy firearms in the 1840s, however, the shield was no longer an effective barrier. Men began to take only its painted cover and medicine attachments into battle. Armed with

this most sacred power of his spirit guardian, a warrior could face the enemy, afraid of nothing, not even his own death.

Those who sought spiritual power were not always successful, and among some Crow and Blackfoot tribes, medicine power could be transferred from one owner to another who had established himself as worthy by proving his personal integrity and forming a respectful relationship with the owner. A young man, perhaps, who desired the proven medicine of an esteemed warrior, might over time develop the relationship of "son" to the medicine owner. The young warrior fostered goodwill by acts of kindness and numerous gifts that demonstrated his generous character. Months might elapse before the transaction was completed. Even then, supernatural powers were involved in shield transfer, and to sustain potency of the shield's power without endangering the original owner required great caution. As in all matters concerning medicine, a set ceremony sanctified the shield and ensured its effectiveness. Above all, this distribution of power in a ritual manner meant more than bestowing prestige on an individual, for the

benefits of protection were shared by the whole tribe when a warrior's fighting strength was increased.

A warrior usually owned a single shield throughout his lifetime, although specific instructions in a dream sometimes empowered him to reproduce a series of shields, usually in multiples of four. No warrior would venture into a sig-nificant undertaking without his protective medicine, which was crucial to his safety, and negligence in handling or caring for his shield could threaten both his physical and spiritual well-being.

Compared to other regalia of the thousands of splendidly attired warriors who roamed the Plains, relatively few shields survived. Some were captured during intertribal fighting or by soldiers as prized trophies in the Indian wars. Inheritance accounted for the disposition of others; when a Crow warrior died, for example, his nearest relative might take on the responsibility of his medicine shield, the more powerful items passing from father to son. A possession of irreplaceable value, central to the warrior's life purpose, the shield usually accompanied him when he died, placed with his body along with other trusted war regalia high on a burial place, where the life-generating sun and sacred winds could bless his departure. Exposed to fierce prairie weather, the physical shield soon disintegrated, but its super-natural powers became free, as did those of the human form, to make the journey to the spirit world.

RED WOODPECKER'S VISION

When Red Woodpecker fasted four days and four nights at a place in Montana called Rimrock-has-no-road, he almost gave up hope of a vision. Then, at dawn on the fifth day, a severe storm broke, and from its midst came a mysterious rider carrying a shield on his back. Attached to the tail of his calico horse was an eagle plume and from its forelock fluttered the wing feather of a hawk. Red Woodpecker could hear the rider singing a medicine song and saw clearly the shield's design of lightning bolts. The rider made the sound of a hawk before he turned and rode away.

Soon another messenger appeared, riding a brown horse, whose neck was painted with the circle of a hawk's nest. "If you paint this shape on your horse," said the spirit, "it will never be shot." His shield showed the figure of a bird with outstretched wings, and clusters of hawk feathers with an eagle-bone whistle hung from its surface.

In his vision Red Woodpecker received five more shields, each one painted with symbolic designs: the perpendicular lines of rain, zigzags of lightning, a crescent moon, and black storm clouds. From this experience he made four lightweight shields, to take on expedition, and three of heavy buffalo hide, which were

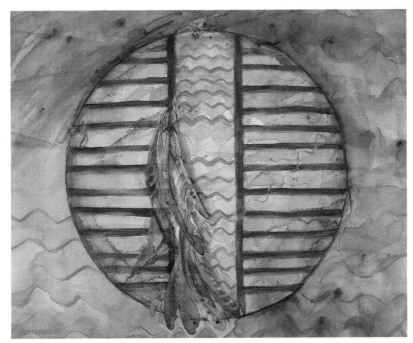

wrapped in painted covers and kept for protection of the home camp. Only the bone whistle and hawk feathers were carried into battle, to honor the spirit messengers who bestowed his powers of immunity in war.

Crow

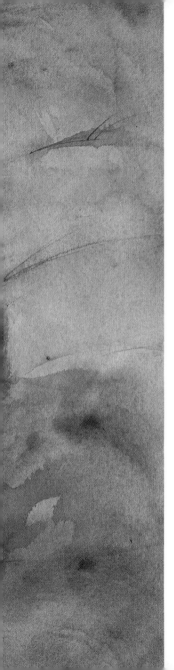

MY HEART IS MANLY

Whenever there is any trouble
I shall not die but get through.
Though arrows are many,
I shall arrive.
My heart is manly.

Crow

LONE MAN'S
DREAM OF THE THUNDERBIRD

*The horsemen in the cloud told me to look down at the
Earth, and said that the sacred stones would guard and
protect me. Before they rode away, they gave me a charm,
which I always carried. If I was in great danger and
escaped alive, I knew it was the charm and sang a song in
its honor. The song relates to the swallow whose flying
precedes a thunderstorm. When I sang my sacred song I
fastened the skin of a swallow on my head. This bird is
so closely related to the Thunderbird that it is honored by
its use. The action of the swallow is very agile. The great-
est aid to a warrior is a good horse, and what a warrior
desires most for his horse is that it may be as swift as the
swallow in dodging the enemy or in direct flight. I sing
this song in honor of the swallow as well as my medicine.*

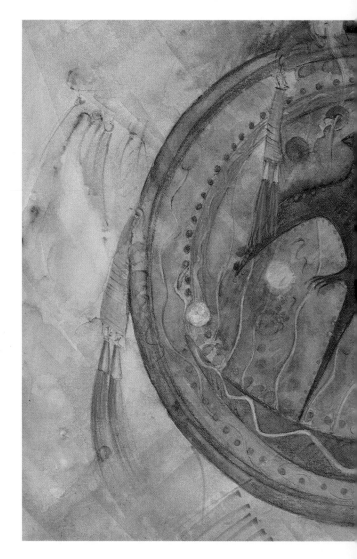

In swift flight

I have sent a swallow nation.

Before the gathering of clouds

In swift flight

My horse like a swallow flying. . . .

Friends, behold!

In a sacred manner

I have been influenced

At the gathering of clouds.

Friends, behold!

Sacred I have been made.

Sioux

SONG OF TURTLE, THE MEDICINE MAN

The Thunder gave me black paint;

He took pity on me.

He gave me black paint; he gave me protection from

harm.

The Thunder makes a noise high up in the air.

The Thunder gave me red paint;

He took pity on me.

He gave me the ability to go through life.

I know this, for I have had a long life.

Cheyenne

THE ORIGIN OF HUMPED-WOLF'S SHIELD

In his vision Humped-Wolf, a Crow warrior, heard something. It was a buffalo bull who changed into a man. Humped-Wolf saw that he wore a horned bonnet with a streamer decorated with eagle feathers, a calf-skin shirt with the hair on it, sleeve holders of buffalo tail, a necklace of buffalo horns between dewclaws. In his hand he held a buffalo tail mounted on a pointed stick, and he was carrying a shield. He was painted white from his nose downward and all over his body. His horse was also painted white, and a plume was tied to the horse's forehead. . . . The buffalo-man said to Humped-Wolf: "Look towards the place where you came from." When he looked he saw many men lined up, all dressed like the buffalo-man, alive. There were also dead people lying all about with guns, bows, and tomahawks. "Look to the West," said the buffalo-man. There, too, he saw many dead people with guns and bows. Then the buffalo-man said: "Tell this to your children and your grandchildren, till there shall be no more fighting. I have given you this medicine. . . . You shall not be driven back by the enemy. I have given you everything that makes a man." When Humped-Wolf arrived back at his camp he told the older men of his vision. "Make it," they said.

Crow

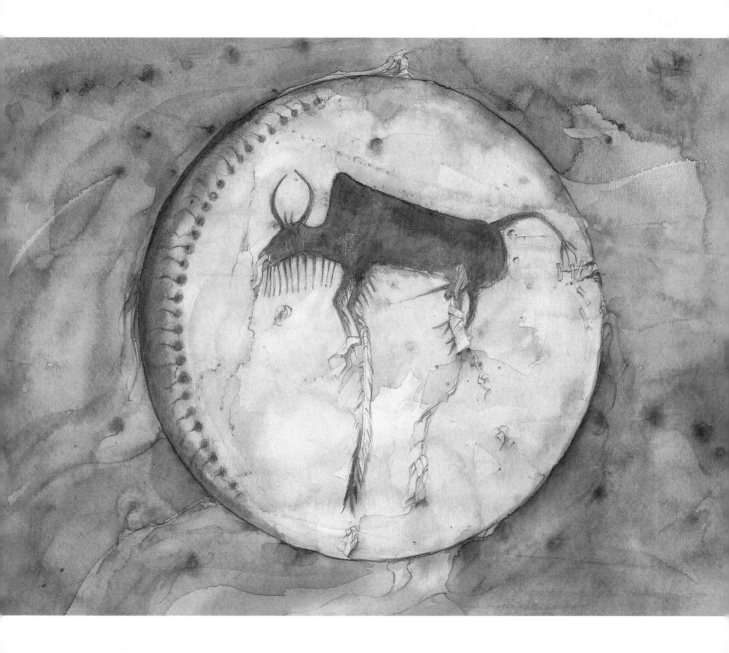

My Grandfather the Sun

I see my Grandfather the Sun; he has medicine power. . . .

My Grandfather gave me the rawhide thong to tie

and the songs to use and the long sinew to tie to the toes.

       My Grandfather, I am tied by medicine power. . . .

       My Grandfather gave me a whistle which has medicine power.

       My Grandfather gave me a tipi; the medicine wind makes it

       rock back and forth on the earth.

My Grandfather gave me a rattle which has medicine power.

My Grandfather gave me the night.

My Grandfather gave me everything on this earth.

Bob-tailed Wolf, Cheyenne

Each Man's Road

The song that I have sung for you is the one
that I sing last in the ceremony, just before dawn.
It means the Eagle, who spreads his wings
and soars above and breathes deep
with the joy of well-being.
The Eagle is myself. . . .

Each man's road is shown to him within his own heart. . . .
He sees all the truths of life and
of the spirit.

Cheyenne

MY SORROWS ARE MANY

You Above, if there be one there who knows
         what is going on,
Repay me today for the distress I have suffered.
Inside the Earth, if there be anyone who knows
         what is going on,
Repay me for the distress I have suffered.

The One Who Causes Things, whoever he be,
I have now had my fill of life.
Grant me death, my sorrows are overabundant.
Though children are timid, they die harsh deaths, it is said.
Though women are timid, you make them die harsh deaths.
I do not want to live long; were I to live long,
My sorrows would be overabundant.
I do not want it.

Crow

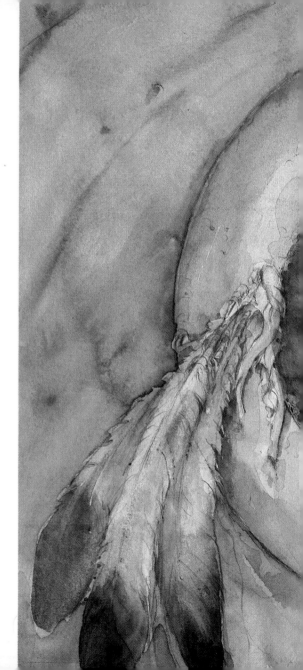

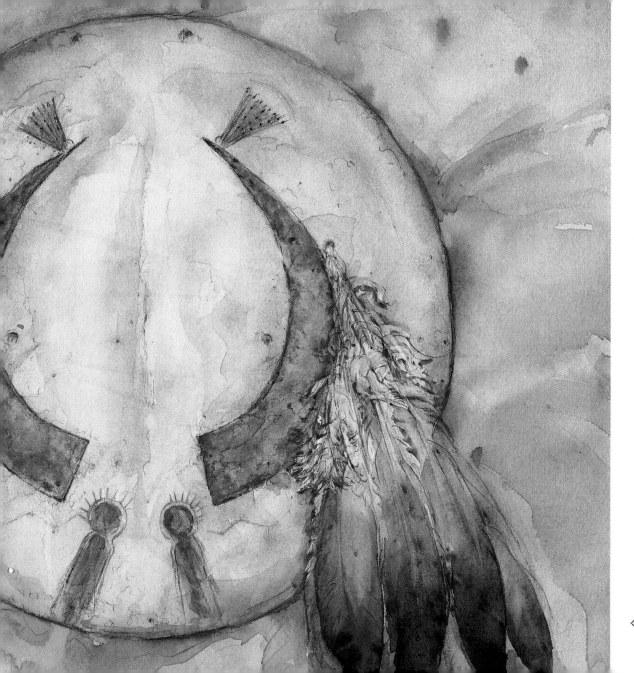

EPILOGUE

◆◆◆◆

The spirits spoke to Black Elk: "Behold the sacred hoop of your people, the grandfathers and the great grandfathers, the younger generations and the older generations. Again they will walk toward a good land. Behold your Eagle—for your nation, like relatives they shall be. Behold the Morning Star—for your nation, like relatives they shall be, and from them they shall have wisdom. Behold the sacred hoop of the world—the people shall stand as one . . . and all living creatures of the earth's generations shall walk together as relatives. All around the universe you have seen the Powers, and they have given you their power. Now you shall go forth to the place you came from. . . . The road of the generations you shall walk. Behold them—this is your nation and you shall go back to them.

Oglala Sioux

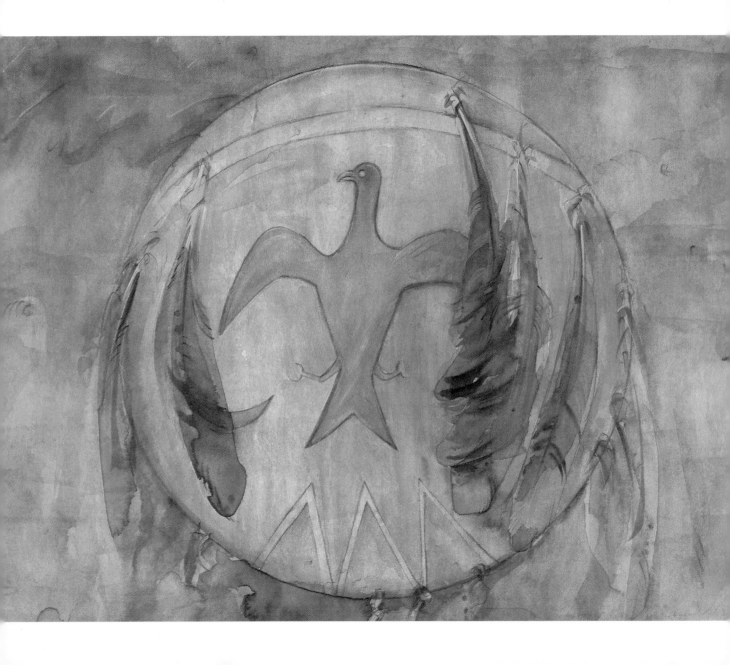

$\mathbf{B}$y the last decade of the nineteenth century, very little remained of Plains Indian culture as it once existed. With the increasing tide of settlers from Europe and the East, tribes were dislocated from their traditional hunting grounds. Buffalo no longer roamed the expansive prairies, and the free, nomadic Plains life was altered irrevocably. The spirit of the buffalo and the spirit of the earth were one, and when the great herds disappeared, so did the native people's sacred connection with the natural world that sustained them. In response to these overwhelming changes, many tribes turned to a new religious movement, desperately searching for spiritual guidance. In the Ghost Dance of 1890, men and women sought visions of their departed relatives, invoking the return of the buffalo herds and the sweet renewal of the earth. Performing songs and ceremonies to restore their former sacred way of life, ghost dancers wore special shirts and dresses painted with protective symbols from the old tribal world that expressed their power to withstand the hardship and disruption of their lives.

During this difficult period of privation, when buffalo hide was no longer available, Ghost Dance shields were made from whatever materials could be found. Even muslin, purchased from traders, was stretched over light wooden hoops, and the dream images painted onto their flimsy surfaces. The power did not lie in the quality of their construction but in their visionary revelations—the mysteries of heaven and earth embodied in the sacred circle. As the symbol of Plains Indian unity and coexistence with natural and spiritual worlds, the sacred hoop of the earth's generations carried a message beyond the limits of time and place.

The medicine shields of Plains warriors were the aesthetic and spiritual manifestations of a tribal reality that continues to hold meaning. Through communion with the powers of the universe, they derived strength and wisdom, and maintained continuity in a world of flux and change. In dreams and visions they found profound themes of inner purpose which gave them personal confidence, confidence in their society and its philosophy, and above all confidence in their own regenerative and cosmic powers. Those who sought the dreams and painted the visions lived in harmony with the natural world and used their environment with respect and resourcefulness. With ultimate skill they followed a way of life that neither destroyed the country nor diminished its spirit, and by their creative genius they have passed on an enduring legacy.

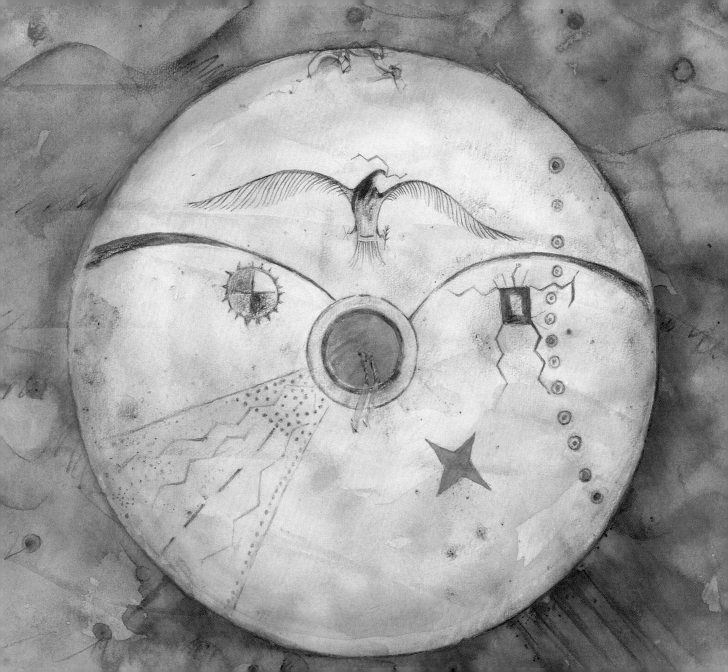

Songs of the Ghost Dance

Father, the Morning Star!
Father, the Morning Star!
Look on us, we have danced until daylight,
Look on us, we have danced until daylight,
Take pity on us.
Take pity on us.

Arapaho

My children, my children,
Here it is, I hand it to you,
The Earth, the Earth.

Arapaho

The Sun's beams are streaming out
The Sun's beams are streaming out
The Sun's yellow rays are running out
The Sun's yellow rays are running out
We shall live again.
We shall live again.

Comanche

SHIELD NOTES

HALF-TITLE

Half-Title. Comanche shield, ca. 1880, approx. 47 cm. diam., Morning Star Gallery, Santa Fe. In common with other Plains tribes, the Comanches believed the sun represented the visible force by which the powers of the universe were revealed.

TABLE OF CONTENTS

Table of Contents. Peigan shield of the Blackfoot Confederacy, ca. 1880, 30 cm., Glenbow Museum, Calgary. Central bird image has brown circles to the lower right, and the top section of light red has two horizontal lines beneath. At the lower edge is sewn a red stroud cut fringe, and the V-trimmed eagle feather is tied with stroud also.

INTRODUCTION

Page 9. Detail from Sioux shield, ca. 1890, Smithsonian Institution, NMNH, Washington, D.C. (See description below for page 43).

Page 10. Kiowa shield, ca. 1880, 44 cm., Smithsonian Institution, NMNH, Washington, D.C. Accessioned in 1884 from a U.S. Army medical museum, this buffalo hide shield and cover once belonged to a Kiowa chief. Blue and yellow were traditional colors used in the sacred ceremonies of the Kiowas.

Page 15. Cheyenne shield, ca. 1870, 48 cm., Denver Art Museum. The sun and the moon, among the greatest of the spiritual powers, are shown with a longhorn steer whose hoof prints mark the four directions of Grandmother Earth.

Page 16–17. Arapaho shield, ca. 1870, 47 cm., Museum für Völkerkunde, Berlin. A crescent moon and the morning star are surrounded by "those that shine at night." Eagle tail feathers are stitched onto a swathe of red stroud, the woolen trade cloth imported from Stroud, England, by the 1860s.

CHAPTER ONE ✳ ✳ ✳

Page 18. Detail from Blackfoot shield, ca. 1850, AMNH, New York. (See description below for pages 32–33).

Page 20–21. Mandan shield cover, ca. 1820, approx. 54 cm., Royal Museum of Scotland, Edinburgh. Attributed to an early tribe of the Upper Missouri River, this hide cover is decorated with a crescent moon, stars, and a single feather. Native earth paints were brown, white, and a yellow ochre, which changed to red after firing.

Page 22–23. Dakota Sioux shield, pre-1850, approx. 47 cm., Colter Bay Indian Arts Museum, Wyoming. Many eagle feathers, scalp locks, and dewclaws adorn this shield, all signifying its owner's special honors in battle, but the design of asymmetrical circles has strictly personal meaning, possibly connected with sacred stones or rocks.

Page 24–25. Sioux shield, pre-1850, approx. 49 cm., Colter Bay Indian Arts Museum, Wyoming. The head of a spectral longhorn steer and various cosmic signs are surrounded by eagle feathers, sacred symbols of a man's war honors.

Page 26. Pawnee shield, ca. 1820, 58.4 cm., British Museum, London. This shield was collected by Duke Paul Wilhelm of Württemberg in 1823 from a Pawnee village at Wolf Fork on the Platte River. Symbols of the sun and moon appear with a horn motif. By this time green pigment, difficult to make, was obtained from traders.

Page 28–29. Arapaho shield, ca. 1860, approx. 52 cm., Morning Star Gallery, Santa Fe. A matching pair of lizards, with lines of power extending from their feet, protected the owner with their ability to disappear from the enemy's sight.

Page 30. Crow shield, pre-1865, approx. 48 cm., Colter Bay Indian Arts Museum, Wyoming. In Crow custom, although offerings were made to the sun, it was most auspicious to receive a vision from the moon, indicating the likelihood of long life. If the owl, chief helper of the moon, appeared to the dreamer, its feathers were attached to the shield or its cover. An eagle plume imparted the power of flight and the ability to silently approach one's prey with keen vision.

Page 32–33. Blackfoot shield, ca. 1850, approx. 47 cm., American Museum of Natural History (AMNH), New York. The sacred buffalo on a red background, the color of life's blood, has circles on each side, possibly depicting a constellation of stars.

Page 34. Comanche shield cover, ca. 1869, approx. 55 cm., Smithsonian Institution, NMNH, Washington, D.C. Around the central circle of blue are motifs of guns and bullets, and eight smoke-black smudge marks, sometimes the symbol of campfires.

Page 36. Kiowa shield, ca. 1820, 50.1 cm., Paul Dyck Research Foundation, Rimrock, Arizona. Attributed to Kiowa chief Dohauson, this shield represents the four sacred mountains and camp circle of the Kiowas.

CHAPTER TWO ***

Page 37. Detail from Sioux shield, ca. 1890, Glenbow Museum, Calgary. (See description below for page 46).

Page 39. Blackfoot shield, ca. 1880, 39 cm., Glenbow Museum, Calgary. This is a shield of the Blood tribe, one of three closely allied tribes of the Blackfoot people. The row of dewclaws, black hair locks, and central image of a buffalo are set in an earthy red. Paint gatherers among the Bloods and North Peigans in Alberta knew the best places to dig for the clay from which pigments were prepared.

Page 43. Sioux shield, ca. 1890, 48.5 cm., Smithsonian Institution, National Museum of Natural History (NMNH), Washington, D.C. The dragonfly represented the power to dart back and forth in battle, which the owner of this shield received in a vision. A row of dewclaws marks the division between day and night, or life and death.

Page 44. Comanche shield cover, ca. 1860, Smithsonian Institution NMNH, Washington, D.C. Collected 1869, Fort Griffin, Texas, by H. M. McElderry, U.S. Army surgeon. Small motifs depict a spider, bears, and buttonlike form, maybe Peyote plant.

Page 46. Sioux shield, ca. 1890, 45.5 cm., Glenbow Museum, Calgary. Made from two discs of rawhide tied with buckskin thonging, this ceremonial shield honors the eagle, a chief representative of thunder, one of the greatest of the powers.

Page 48–49. Crow shield cover, ca. 1860, 60 cm., Heye Foundation of the American Indian, New York. A Crow chief named Pretty Bear once carried this shield. Two eagles and stars on either side of a moon figure were protecting patrons of its owner.

Page 51. Kiowa shield, pre-1880, 48 cm., Smithsonian Institution, NMNH, Washington, D.C. Collected from Indian Territory, Oklahoma, this Tai-me shield may once have belonged to a keeper of the sacred figurine of the Kiowa Sun Dance. The Tai-me, the central personage in this ceremony of the world's renewal, bore symbols of the sun and moon upon its face, breast, and back.

Page 52. Crow shield, ca. 1850, approx. 44 cm., Morning Star Gallery, Santa Fe. Two bears, male and female, pose face to face, with zigzag lines of supernatural power coming from their ferocious jaws.

Page 54–55. Blackfoot shield, pre-1840, 51 cm., Southwest Museum, Los Angeles. Alexander Acevedo Collection. Reputedly collected from a Blackfoot chief in 1846, this shield probably depicts the Thunderbird, the great bird with the power to make rain and lightning, and to cause the crash of a thunderstorm with the flap of its huge wings.

Page 56. Crow shield, ca. 1860, 57 cm., Field Museum, Chicago. The two halves of this design may symbolize earth and sky, with a female bear attacking another in whose jaws a human hand appears. Bear ears were attached to ensure power against the enemy and to honor this awesome benefactor from a vision.

Page 58–59. Crow shield cover, ca. 1860, 51 cm., Field Museum, Chicago. The morning star, crescent moon, and two dragonflies with power lines are set against a dark sky, indicating the owner's special connection with the powers.

CHAPTER THREE ✧ ✧ ✧

Page 60. Detail from Sioux shield, ca 1890, Glenbow Museum, Calgary. (See description below for pages 70–71.)

Page 63. Crow shield, ca. 1860, 55 cm., Museum für Völkerkunde, Berlin. A single bear's paw dominates this shield, which has a mummified weasel concealed among owl and eagle feathers. Of all Plains animals, the bear was most revered for its great strength and ferocity, and also for its long, powerful claws, which were adept at rooting out plants valued by Plains people for their healing properties. Received in a vision, this image of a bear endowed the warrior with its supernatural power.

Page 65. Crow shield, ca. 1860, 51 cm., Museum für Völkerkunde, Berlin. Collected by Fred Harvey in

1905, this design closely resembles one in the Chicago Field Museum (see page 65) with red and white divisions, bears engaged in confrontation, and the attachment of a bear's ear.

Page 67. Crow shield, pre-1850, approx. 47 cm., Colter Bay Indian Arts Museum, Wyoming. Worn and fragile, this design, with zigzags and bold lines, may signify the dramatic storm conditions that accompanied the owner's vision.

Page 68–69. Crow shield, pre-1850, 56 cm., Heye Foundation, New York. Said to have belonged once to Chief Eelapuash; the central figure is believed to represent the moon, an auspicious patron in Crow tradition.

Page 70–71. Sioux dance shield, ca. 1890, 44.5 cm., Glenbow Museum, Calgary. Made of hide sewn over a wooden hoop, this shield was for ceremonial use. Ornamented with tin cones, dyed red porcupine quills, horsehair, and feathers, the central motif is a large bird with forked tail, probably the Thunderbird.

Page 72–73. Northern Cheyenne shield, ca. 1860, 51 cm., Smithsonian Institution, NMNH, Washington, D.C. The turtle, symbol of the earth, was associated with longevity and endurance. Considered a sacred gift from Grandmother Earth, blue paint that turned green on smoke-tanned buckskin began to appear about 1830, its source a closely guarded secret. After their 1840 treaty with the Comanches and Kiowas, the Cheyennes began trading the blue pigment with their new allies, but its origin remained a secret.

Page 75. Crow shield, ca. 1860, 52 cm., Field Museum, Chicago. Made by a Crow warrior, Bull That Goes Hunting, from his vision of a huge buffalo bull strong enough to withstand a hail of bullets, this shield was probably used in battle. The green border on the left may signify summer, the preferred season for war parties.

Page 76. Cheyenne shield, ca. 1860, 46 cm., Smithsonian Institution, NMNH, Washington, D.C. The sun, moon, the sacred hills, and a mysterious horned creature emanating spirit power are surrounded by eagle feathers on red stroud.

Page 79. Southern Cheyenne shield, pre-1850, 49 cm., Detroit Institute of Arts. Around the central Thunderbird fly smaller birds with powers of swiftness and agility. Above lies the crescent moon, and below the seven stars or Pleiades. This shield, which once belonged to Little Rock, Chief Black Kettle's second-in-command, was captured by General Custer at the battle of the Wachita in 1868.

Page 80–81. Crow shield, ca. 1860, 55 cm., Museum für Völkerkunde, Berlin. Collected by Fred Harvey, this heavy hide shield shows the horns of a buffalo, whose sacred powers ensured the life force of Plains culture until the 1890s.

EPILOGUE ❖ ❖ ❖

Page 82. Detail from Arapaho shield, ca. 1890, Portland Art Museum, Oregon. (See description below for page 89).

Page 84. Cheyenne shield, ca. 1890, 45 cm., Southwest Museum, Los Angeles. Alexander Acevedo Collection. Painted muslin stretched over a wooden hoop was one of the only ways to make a shield after the buffalo were gone. This Ghost Dance shield was collected on the Canadian River in Oklahoma in 1891, a last reminder of the spiritual endurance of the Plains Indians.

Page 87. Kiowa shield, c. 1890, 51 cm., Smithsonian Institution, NMNH, Washington, D. C. Victor J. Evans collection; acceded in 1931. The large bird with powerful wings and a cornstalk held in one claw is shown with traditional symbols of Kiowa power.

Page 89. Arapaho shield, ca. 1890, 39 cm., Portland Art Museum, Oregon. Elizabeth Cole Butler Collection. Painted with images of antelope, turtle, sun, and moons, this small hide shield was made for the Ghost Dance to recall old-time lifeways.

BIBLIOGRAPHY

Arapaho Prayer. "Listen All You Creatures," *The Wind River Rendezvous*. Reprint. Wyoming: Saint Stephen's Indian Mission Foundation.

Curtis, Edward S. *The North American Indian,* vols. 3-4. Cambridge, Mass.: University Press, 1908-09.

Curtis, Natalie. *The Indians' Book: Songs and Legends of the American Indians.* 1907. Reprint. New York: Dover Publications, 1968.

DeMallie, Raymond J., ed. *The Sixth Grandfather: Black Elk's Teachings Given to John G. Neihardt.* Lincoln: University of Nebraska Press, 1984.

Densmore, Frances. *Cheyenne and Arapaho Music: Southwest Museum Papers 10.* Los Angeles: Southwest Museum,1936.

——. *Teton Sioux Music.* Smithsonian Institution, Bureau of American Ethnology Bulletin no. 61, Washington, D.C., 1918.

Dyck, Paul. "The Plains Shield." *American Indian Art Magazine* 1, no. 1 (1975), pp. 34-41.

Erdoes, Richard, and Alfonso Ortiz. *American Indian Myths and Legends.* New York: Pantheon Books, 1983.

Ewers, John C. *Plains Indian Painting.* Stanford, Calif.: Stanford University Press, 1939.

Fletcher, Alice C. *The Hako: A Pawnee Ceremony.* Bureau of American Ethnology, 22nd Annual Report Part II, 1900-1901.

Gibbs, Peter. "Duke Paul Wilhelm Collection in the British Museum," *American Indian Art Magazine* 7, no. 3 (1982.), pp. 52-61.

Grinnell, George B. *Blackfoot Lodge Tales.* 1893. Reprint. Lincoln: University of Nebraska Press, 1962.

Kan, Michael, and W. Wierzbowski. "Notes on an Important Southern Cheyenne Shield," *Bulletin of the Detroit Institute of Arts 57,* no. 3 (1979.), pp. 125-133.

Kroeber, A. L. *The Arapaho.* American Museum of Natural History Bulletin no. 18, New York, 1902-1907.

Lowie, Robert H. *The Religion of the Crow Indians.* American Museum of Natural History Anthropological Papers, no. 25, pp. 309-444. (New York: Part 1, 1918; part 2, 1922) pp. 1-308; 309-444.

——. *Crow Prayers.* American Anthropologist 35. American Anthropological Association, 1933.

Marriott, Alice. *Kiowa Years: A Study in Culture Impact.* MacMillan McGraw Publishing Co., 1968.

Mooney, James. *The Ghost Dance Religion.* Smithsonian Institution, Bureau of American Ethnology Bulletin no. 14 (Washington, D.C., 1893).

McClintock, Walter. *The Old North Trail.* Lincoln: University of Nebraska Press, 1977.

McCoy, Ronald. "Circles of Power." *Plateau 55* (1984), pp. 1-32.

Powell, Peter J. "Beauty for New Life: Cheyenne and Lakota Sacred Art." In *Native American Heritage.* ed. Evan M. Maurer. Chicago: Art Institute of Chicago (1977), pp. 33-56.

Schlesier, Karl H. *The Wolves of Heaven: Cheyenne Shamanism, Ceremonies, and Prehistoric Origins.* Norman: University of Oklahoma Press, 1987.

Standing Bear, Luther. *Land of the Spotted Eagle.* Houghton Mifflin, 1933.

Walker, James R. *Lakota Belief and Ritual.* Ed. Raymond J. DeMallie and Elaine A. Jahner. Lincoln: University of Nebraska Press, 1980.

—————. *The Sun Dance and Other Ceremonies of the Oglala Sioux.* American Museum of Natural History Anthropological Papers, no. 16, New York, 1917.

Walters, Anna Lee. *Spirit of Native America.* San Francisco: Chronicle Books, 1989.

Weltfish, Gene. *The Lost Universe: Pawnee Life and Culture.* Lincoln: University of Nebraska Press, 1977.

Wildschut, William. *Crow Indian Medicine Bundles.* Ed. by John C. Ewers. New York: Heye Foundation, 1975.

Wissler, Clark. *Ceremonial Bundles of the Blackfoot Indians.* American Museum of Natural History Anthropological Papers, no. 7, part 2. (New York, 1912), pp. 65-289.

ENDNOTES

Table of Contents. Frances Densmore, *Teton Sioux Music*, Smithsonian Institution, Bureau of American Ethnology Bulletin, No. 61 (Washington, D.C., 1918), p. 186.

Page 10. James Walker, *The Sun Dance and Other Ceremonies of the Oglala Sioux*, American Museum of Natural History Anthropological Papers, No. 16 (New York, 1917), p. 160.

Page 14. Frances Densmore, Washington, D.C., 1918, p. 99.

Page 16. A. L. Kroeber, *The Arapaho*, American Museum of Natural History Bulletin, No. 18 (New York, 1902–1907), p. 313.

Page 19. Told by Letakots-Lesa (Eagle Chief) in Natalie Curtis, *The Indians' Book* (1907; reprint, New York: Dover Publications, 1968), p. 98.

Page 20. Karl H. Schlesier, *The Wolves of Heaven: Cheyenne Shamanism, Ceremonies and Prehistoric Origins* (Norman: University of Oklahoma Press, 1987), pp. 12–13.

page 21. Chief Luther Standing Bear, *Land of the Spotted Eagle* (Boston: Houghton Mifflin, 1933), p. xix.

Page 23. Frances Densmore, Washington, D.C., 1918, p. 172.

Page 24–25. James Walker, pp. 158–161.

page 27. Alice C. Fletcher, *The Hako: A Pawnee Ceremony*, Smithsonian Institution, Bureau of American Ethnology 22nd Annual Report Part II (Washington, D.C., 1900–1901), pp. 128–30.

Page 28. Benjamin Friday and William Shakespeare of the Wind River Reservation, Saint Stephen's Indian Mission, Wyoming.

Page 31. Robert H. Lowie, *The Religion of the Crow Indians*, American Museum of Natural History Anthropological Papers, No. 25 (New York, 1922), pp. 427–28.

Page 33. Clark Wissler, *Ceremonial Bundles of the Blackfoot Indians*, American Museum of Natural History Anthropological Papers, No. 7 (New York, 1912), p. 253.

Page 35. Extracted from the Comanche leader's speech at the Medicine Lodge Council, 1867, addressed to the Peace Commissioner. *Great Documents in Indian History*, eds. Wayne Moquin and C. Van Doren, Praeger Publishers (New York, 1973), p. 209.

Page 36. James Mooney, *The Ghost Dance Religion*, Smithsonian Institution, Bureau of American Ethnology 14th Annual Report Part II (Washington, D.C., 1892–93), p. 319.

Page 38. G. B. Grinnell, *Blackfoot Lodge Tales* (1893; reprint, Lincoln: University of Nebraska Press, 1962), pp. 141–42.

Page 41. Lame Deer, *American Indian Myths and Legends*, Eds. Richard Erdoes and Alfonso Ortiz (New York, Pantheon Books, 1983), p. 72.

Page 42. James R. Walker, *Lakota Belief and Ritual*, eds. Raymond J. DeMallie and Elaine A. Jahner (Lincoln: University of Nebraska Press, 1980), p. 79.

Page 45. Frances Densmore, Washington, D.C., 1918, pp. 181–83.

Page 47. Edward Curtis, *The North American Indian*, vol. 3 (Cambridge, Mass.: University Press, 1908), p. 77.

Page 49. Robert H. Lowie, *The Myths and Traditions of the Crow Indians*, American Museum of Natural History Anthropological Papers, No. 25 (New York, 1918), pp. 56–72.

Page 50. Alice Marriott, *Kiowa Years: A Study in Culture Impact* (New York: MacMillan McGraw, 1968), p. 118.

Page 53. Robert H. Lowie, New York, 1918, p. 183.

Page 55. Clark Wissler, pp. 252–53.

Page 57. Edward Curtis, *The North American Indian*, vol. 4 (Cambridge, Mass.: University Press, 1909), p. 98.

Page 58. *Ibid.*, p. 53.

Page 61. Told by Chief Maza Blask, Oglala Sioux, to Natalie Curtis, *The Indians' Book* (1907; reprint, New York: Dover Publications, 1968), pp. 38–39.

Page 66–67. W. Wildschut, *Crow Indian Medicine Bundles*, Heye Foundation (New York, 1975), pp. 68–70.

Page 69. Robert H. Lowie, New York, 1922, p. 410.

Page 71. Frances Densmore, Washington, D.C., 1918, pp. 161–65.

Page 72. Frances Densmore, *Cheyenne and Arapaho Music*, Southwest Museum Papers, No. 10 (Los Angeles, 1936), p. 64.

Page 74. Robert H. Lowie, New York, 1922, pp. 409–10.

Page 77. Frances Densmore, Los Angeles, 1936, p. 56.

Page 78. Told by Cheyenne leader *Mowihaiz* (Magpie) to Natalie Curtis, *The Indians' Book*, (1907; reprint, New York: Dover Publications, 1968), pp. 164–65.

Page 80. R. H. Lowie, "Crow Prayers," *American Anthropologist* 35 (1933), p. 442.

Page 83. From the original Black Elk transcript in Raymond DeMallie, ed., *The Sixth Grandfather: Black Elk's Teachings Given to John G. Neihardt* (Lincoln: University of Nebraska Press, 1984), pp. 125–41.

Page 88. James Mooney, p. 984 and p. 1046.

FEB 0   2009